THE WORLD OF AUTOMOBILES

Hop Inside the Most Exotic Cars

Written by Norm Geddis

The World of Automobiles

Carmakers from Around the Globe

Concept Cars: Past and Future

Customizing Your Ride

Hop Inside the Most Exotic Cars

Toughest Trucks from the Streets to Showtime

THE WORLD OF AUTOMOBILES

Hop Inside the Most Exotic Cars

Written by Norm Geddis

MC

MASON CREST

Mason Crest
450 Parkway Drive, Suite D
Broomall, Pennsylvania 19008
(866) MCP-BOOK (toll free)

First printing
9 8 7 6 5 4 3 2 1

ISBN (hardback) 978-1-4222-4090-8
ISBN (series) 978-1-4222-4086-1
ISBN (ebook) 978-1-4222-7709-6

Library of Congress Cataloging-in-Publication Data

Names: Geddis, Norm, author.
Title: Hop inside the most exotic cars / Norm Geddis.
Description: Broomall, Pennsylvania : Mason Crest, [2019] | Series: The world
    of automobiles | Includes bibliographical references and index.
Identifiers: LCCN 2018018048 (print) | LCCN 2018019230 (ebook) | ISBN
9781422277096 (eBook) | ISBN 9781422240908 (hardback) | ISBN
9781422240861(series)
Subjects: LCSH: Sports cars--Juvenile literature.
Classification: LCC TL236 (ebook) | LCC TL236 .G39 2019 (print) | DDC
    629.222--dc23
LC record available at https://lccn.loc.gov/2018018048

Developed and Produced by National Highlights Inc.
Editor: Andrew Luke
Interior and cover design: Annalisa Gumbrecht, Studio Gumbrecht
Production: Michelle Luke

NATIONAL
HIGHLIGHTS

QR CODES AND LINKS TO THIRD-PARTY CONTENT

CONTENTS

KEY ICONS TO LOOK FOR:

 Words to understand: These words with their easy-to-understand definitions will increase the reader's understanding of the text while building vocabulary skills.

 Sidebars: This boxed material within the main text allows readers to build knowledge, gain insights, explore possibilities, and broaden their perspectives by weaving together additional information to provide realistic and holistic perspectives.

 Educational videos: Readers can view videos by scanning our QR codes, providing them with additional educational content to supplement the text. Examples include news coverage, moments in history, speeches, iconic sports moments, and much more!

 Text-dependent questions: These questions send the reader back to the text for more careful attention to the evidence presented there.

 Research projects: Readers are pointed toward areas of further inquiry connected to each chapter. Suggestions are provided for projects that encourage deeper research and analysis.

 Series of glossary of key terms: This back-of-the-book glossary contains terminology used throughout this series. Words found here increase the reader's ability to read and comprehend higher-level books and articles in this field.

aerodynamics
the qualities of an object that affect how easily it is able to move through the air

exotic
having a strange or bizarre allure, beauty, or quality

horsepower
a unit of measurement of the power of an engine

mystique
an aura of mystery or mystical power

vintage
representing the high quality of a past time

CHAPTER 1

Cars Few Can Possess

There is a well-kept secret people should know. Those sleek and ultra-cool vehicles taking movie heroes and villains to and from **exotic** locales—they really do exist. And vehicles as amazing as ones out of Hollywood blockbusters are as close as the next car moving down the road.

Just like vehicles in the fantastical and weird world of imagination, the exotic automobiles that exist today inspire thrills, shock value, excitement, sometimes a little bit of risk, and even some fear. Does that sentence seem at all exaggerated? Maybe at first glance. But delving a little deeper into the world of exotic cars reveals some truly fascinating and beautiful machines. These cars have names

A vintage high-end convertible on display at the Saratoga Automobile Museum, in Saratoga, NY.

like Lamborghini, Aston Martin, and Maybach. Additionally, these cars also have a direct relationship with everyday carmakers like Ford, Honda, and Toyota.

Very few of these high-end cars are sold in showrooms. Owning one requires a great deal of money and is viewed by many as a symbol of one's personal achievement.

Automakers like Ford, Honda, Toyota, GM and Chrysler sell more than one hundred thousand vehicles each month. Others like Hyundai, Kia, Audi, and Volvo sell tens of thousands of vehicles a month. The automakers featured in this book will sell as few as a handful of cars a year, but no more than a few thousand. As can be imagined, these cars cost in excess of $100,000, with many bearing a price tag of more than one million dollars.

These automobiles cost a fortune—literally. Owning an exotic car can cost tens of thousands of dollars per year to maintain and protect. Only specially trained mechanics are qualified to work on these cars. So expensive and sought after are some of these vehicles that owners must pay special, heightened attention to security, both at home and on the road. Typically, these cars almost never find their way into the neighborhood grocery store parking lot for fear of dings, scratches, and even theft.

Why do people spend so much money on these cars? And who buys them?

Beyoncé and husband Jay-Z are pop and rap music icons who appreciate the finer things in life, including Rolls-Royce and Bugatti automobiles.

Let's start with something important to know about cars. They transform the people riding in them. In a fast-moving car, humans become something that for thousands of years they only dreamt of—the fastest creatures on Earth. The feeling of speed turns riders into powerful travelers, free to go wherever the roads can take them.

When someone has earned or amassed a great deal of wealth, buying an exotic car or two makes them travelers with swagger and high style. Many celebrities love using exotic cars to add to their glamour and **mystique**. Several exotic cars have made cameos in popular music videos and during on-stage performances. Famous people and show business personalities also like to collect flashy cars and display them proudly. Many of today's and yesterday's professional athletes are known for their taste in stylish, exotic cars.

Jay-Z and Beyoncé love glamour; and along with abundant talent, their style sense helped them become a music power couple. Their love of the finer things definitely shows in their taste for exotic rides. A gift from her husband on her 25th birthday, Beyoncé became the owner of a rare **vintage** 1959 Rolls-Royce Silver Cloud II Convertible. This sublime Rolls is worth around $1 million (US).

Another musician who likes to show off his Rolls is rapper Gucci Mane. He prefers a sporty red Rolls-Royce Dawn with red interior, a convertible unique to the Rolls-Royce brand.

Not to be outdone in the fabulous gift department, Beyoncé gifted her husband a gorgeous Bugatti Veyron Super Sport. Some other celebrities also are known to own this particular Bugatti. These people include New England Patriot Tom Brady and boxer Floyd Mayweather, Jr.

However, both of these amazing cars pale in comparison to one particular supercar, rumored to have been purchased

Superstar athletes quarterback Tom Brady and boxer Floyd Mayweather, Jr. are each said to be owners of a Bugatti Veyron.

by Jay-Z. In his video for "Lost One," Jay-Z is seen leaving his New York apartment and getting into an $8-million-dollar Maybach Excelero. A debate has been going on in popular media and on the Internet ever since about whether Jay-Z actually purchased an Excelero. So far, Jay-Z himself is keeping quiet. A possible explanation is that Mercedes, the owner of the Maybach brand, lent Jay-Z the car for the video shoot. This is a common practice so supercar automakers can get publicity by showing their cars alongside superstars. Either way, Jay-Z and the Excelero look sharp.

WHAT IS A MAKE AND MODEL?

Cars are usually referred to by their make and model, such as: Toyota (make) Corolla (model). The make is usually the auto company's name and the model is the brand name of the car. An example of an exotic car make and model would the Bugatti (make) Veyron (model).

The Quattroporte is the flagship car for Italian carmaker Maserati.

The Maserati Quattroporte has been in production since 1963. It is Maserati's flagship car. Many European soccer stars drive the Quattroporte. Here in the United States, Felix Hernandez of the Seattle Mariners is also the proud owner of a Quattroporte. The parent company of Maserati, Fiat Chrysler Automobiles, has made an effort in recent years to sell more Maserati cars in America. The car comes with a choice of a 3.0L, 404-horsepower V6 or an even more powerful 3.8L, 523-horsepower V8. Both engines could give Beyoncé's Rolls-Royce Silver Cloud a run for its money.

The Bentley Continental is the car that clearly shows off luxury. It's hard to say which car sits at the pinnacle of luxury. The Rolls-Royce? Aston Martin? Bentley? But it's certainly up there at the top. Bentley has manufactured the Continental every year since 1952. The GT version of the Continental weighs two and a half tons. Buyers have a choice between a 4.0L turbocharged V8 or a 6.0L turbocharged V12. Tennis star Serena Williams owns one of these beautiful Continental GTs. If she wants, Ms. Williams can go from 0 to 60 mph in four seconds.

The Lamborghini Gallardo is the company's top seller of all time. The car was available for purchase between 2004 and 2014. The Gallardo was a little less powerful than its new cousin, the Aventador. But with a maximum of 562 ear-splitting **horsepower**, the car is still a powerhouse. Retired basketball star Shaquille O'Neal owns a Lamborghini Gallardo. The 5.2L V10 engine can go from 0 to 60 in 3.4 seconds.

The Gallardo is the best-selling Lamborghini model of all time.

Drive California canyon country from the front seat of a Ferrari 430.

Lamborghini is one of the world's best-known exotic sports car makers. The Aventador is one of Lamborghini's more recent offerings, after the Huracan and the Centenario (still in production as of 2017). Five thousand Aventadors have been sold since the brand launched in 2011. One of those was sold to Los Angeles Laker Kobe Bryant. The car comes with a blazing 6.5L V12 engine. With 690 horsepower, the car is well justified in having a 7-speed transmission. Get in this baby and go 0 to 60 in 2.9 seconds.

The Ferrari F430 was built from 2004 to 2009. A 4.3L V8 engine gives this car 491 horsepower that reaches speeds of more than 300 mph. NBA star LeBron James and pro football player Reggie Bush each own one of these elegant Italian beauties.

The McLaren is Britain's answer to Italian sports cars. The car came into production in 2011, the same year as the Lamborghini Aventador. Formula One race car driver Lewis Hamilton drives one of these when he's motoring on regular roads.

NBA superstar LeBron James is the owner of a Ferrari F430.

The influence of exotic cars extends beyond the rich and famous (or just plain rich). The designers of these cars influence the entire auto industry. Innovations in body design, the engineering of how a car looks, and how the body adds to performance come from the top-tier engineers who are the ones that create these amazing cars.

Back in the 1950s, race car makers started experimenting with **aerodynamics**. Aerodynamics is the branch of mechanics that deals with the motion of air and the effects of such motion on bodies in the medium.

The makers of these cars discovered that air travels faster around curves, so a car with more rounded surfaces faces less drag from the wind. Drag is the measurement of the aerodynamic force exerted on a vehicle that tends to reduce its forward motion. By reducing drag, a car travels faster. The lower the drag, the less fuel a car burns.

Ever since the 1960s when the second generation of exotic automobiles came to prominence after World War II, exotic cars have led the way in car design.

Take a look at any of the Lamborghini models produced around 2007. The bodies are already very angular. They become even more angular over the next decade. Over the last ten years, Lamborghini bodies have become cut like diamonds, with each new model having more and more shaped angles constructed into the body. This was done because today's computer models show that these angles decrease drag over the curved shape most cars had in the last decades of the twentieth century. The 1980s and 1990s were the first decades where computer models helped design automobiles.

Now compare the Lamborghini of today to the 2017 Honda Civic. Today's Civic looks a little like a Lamborghini with shaped, or what are called faceted, angles cut into the body.

The design of the 2017 Honda Civic is influenced by that of a Lamborghini.

The Civic from 2007 has a curvier design. This demonstrates how the design of so called supercars influences the design of everyday automobiles.

Of course, the supercar projects attract the best designers and engineers, and they get to test their best ideas on these vehicles. The result is that ideas that are proven to improve performance, comfort, and ease of use get adopted throughout the automotive industry.

The story of the exotic automobile is a story of perseverance, innovation, and a little bit of luck. Some of these exotic car companies started out of a garage; others were planned at the highest levels of industry. And a few times throughout the brief history of automobiles, the guy or gal working out of the garage (women invented the turn signal and windshield wiper) got the better of the world's top car companies.

Many exotic cars are planned at the highest levels of the industry, but sometimes they are the startup idea of new and innovative designers.

1. True or false: increased drag helps a car moves faster.

2. How do exotic car designers influence the common carmakers?

3. How do exotic car makers sometimes get publicity for their cars?

RESEARCH PROJECT

The 24 Hours of Le Mans race in France has been held every year since 1923, making it the oldest endurance race in the world. Research the 1959 Le Mans race and discover how the life of one of the winning drivers transformed American car design. Write a four-hundred-word report on the story.

WORDS TO UNDERSTAND

Great Depression
the period between 1929 and the beginning of World War II when most of the world's developed countries were experiencing a long economic downturn

new money
also known as nouveau riche, this term refers to people with a fortune only recently acquired

old money
wealth inherited from generation to generation, especially wealth that confers status and social acceptance

street-legal
a car that conforms to all the local and national laws and regulations allowing it to be driven on public roads

CHAPTER 2

Pre-World War II: Luxury Overkill

All fairy tales begin with the words, "Once upon a time . . ."
This part of the story of exotic cars is very much like a fairy tale
and begins like every other fairy tale. However, in this case, the
ending is not a happy one. That's because this car tale ends
at the beginning of World War II. Still, the story of the grand
luxury automobiles of this period is important to understanding
the racing culture that evolved after World War II.

So . . .

Looking back at pre-WWII automobiles helps to explain the rise of exotic cars.

Once upon a time in America and Europe, the industrial revolution was creating a new type of rich person. Before this period, most people were rich because they had inherited their wealth from their parents. There was a lot of **old money,** and **new money** had been difficult to find. But then, as industry rose, these newly rich people made their money by building and owning factories. These factories made everything from apple peelers to canned yams. The old money people made up primarily of agricultural landowners and, in Europe, royalty, tended to look down on the new money people.

Watch a newsreel on the 1933 24 Hours of Le Mans race.

The new money desired a way to show off their wealth and new found social importance, setting them apart from the old money. They gravitated toward the greatest and newest of all machines, the horseless carriage (later called the automobile). The older wealthy class thought horseless carriages to be noisy, dirty, and something civilized people didn't own or use. The old rich class tended to scoff at new money's desire to transcend the old world's staid tradition of refined travel. These newly rich folks were seeking newfangled, wild thrills by throttling down the road at 35 mph or more—the ultimate new experience that cars made possible.

This was roughly the period between the early 1900s and **The Great Depression**, which began when the financial markets crashed in 1929. From the turn of the twentieth century into the years of The Great Depression, the successful and adventurous carmakers poured money into ever faster and more elegant cars.

First came the race car, which was not intended for use on the road. Pretty soon racing enthusiasts were demanding versions they could buy and drive on open roads. While racing was becoming a popular sport, it was expensive to travel to races, participate in pre-race promotions, and maintain vehicles. Making versions of their racing cars to sell to the public became a revenue source for racing teams. A win at a big race meant that the carmaker's **street-legal** versions would be in high demand.

In addition to their race cars, these same carmakers later put the same racing engines and super rugged chassis on cars loaded with lots of luxury. These were big and beautiful looking cars with leather interiors and plush seats. What began as a search for speed led to the emergence of the most visually beautiful cars ever created.

Here are a few of the treasures from this period:

Rolls-Royce

Almost everyone has heard of Rolls-Royce. More than any other carmaker, Rolls-Royce holds the spot in everyone's imagination as the car rich people own. A marketing study done in 1987 showed that only Coca-Cola was a more

Rolls-Royce is one of the world's most recognizable luxury brands.

recognized brand than Rolls-Royce. Although this may not still be true today, Rolls-Royce is still a highly regarded and well-known luxury brand. In terms of how it operates, Rolls-Royce has been several different companies in the past and is currently divided into two companies—Rolls-Royce Holdings and Rolls-Royce Motor Cars. The former makes airplane engines. The latter is today's carmaker.

Rolls-Royce began as a partnership between a race car maker and a car dealer. It turned out the partnership struck the perfect balance. Rolls-Royce was the first luxury carmaker to attract both old money and new money.

Rolls-Royce didn't exactly start out with the intention of making world-class luxury cars. The partnership was formed in 1904 between Henry Royce and Charles Rose. Henry Royce was already making two cylinder racers, and Charles Rose already owned a successful car dealership.

The first Rolls-Royce cars were small 10-to-30 horsepower two-seater motor carriages. Their style was more horse carriage than automobile. The first model, the Rolls-Royce 10hp, premiered at the Paris Auto Show (then called the Paris Automobile Salon) in 1904. The Paris Auto Show still takes place every other year.

The first thing buyers noticed about the Rolls was how quiet the motor ran. The quiet motor had an appeal to Europe's old money, who wanted something more refined and better quality than most everybody else. Prior to cars like the Rolls, automobiles were thought to be "gauche," or lacking in social grace, and therefore not suitable for the sophisticated people of society. This was in part because of the noise they made. Simply stated, Rolls-Royce made owning an automobile appealing to rich people with particular tastes.

This crossover where Rolls-Royce appealed to just about

everyone was accomplished by the man who was called the "hyphen" in Rolls-Royce. In a very real sense, this was true. Much to the company's credit, they employed a man named Claude Johnson. His job was primarily to oversee the company and plan for its future. It was Johnson who saw the potential of Rolls-Royce as the automaker of the rich and powerful. So at his urging, Rolls-Royce dropped their race car line of automobiles.

The first Rolls-Royce luxury car was the Silver Ghost. In production from 1906 to 1926, a total of almost eight thousand were made in both the United Kingdom and at a Rolls-Royce plant in Springfield, MA. The engine was a huge 7.4L straight 6, meaning its six cylinders are set in a straight line.

Today, the Silver Ghosts still on the road are considered the most valuable cars in existence, valued more than $35 million for a car in top condition.

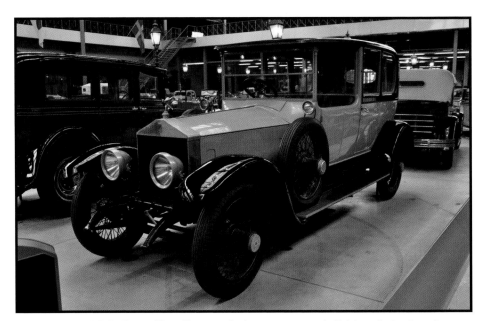

A 1921 Rolls-Royce Silver Ghost on display at a museum in Belgium. A street-ready version of this car that is in top condition would be worth more than $30 million.

Sultan Hassanal Bolkiah of Brunei holds the Guinness World Record for both the largest car collection and largest collection of Rolls-Royce automobiles. His collection totals around five thousand cars, ten percent of which are Rolls-Royces. Other cars in the collection include more than one hundred specially made Mercedes and dozens of Aston Martins.

Queen Elizabeth II of the United Kingdom was a trained mechanic who worked on ambulances during World War II. She bought her first car in 1950, a Rolls-Royce Phantom IV. Her cars today include several Bentleys, an Aston Martin, and two Range Rovers that she uses to drive around her castle property in Scotland.

Bugatti

Bugatti has already been mentioned as one of the cars Jay-Z and Beyoncé have in their car collection. But today's Bugatti is not the same as the Bugatti car company of the early twentieth century. Today's Bugatti is a revival of the name. The original company

A museum in California displays a 1932 edition of the Bugatti Type 55, the company's first street-legal model.

A racer like this classic Bugatti Type 51 won the 1933 Monaco Grand Prix.

was a family-owned business, founded in Germany by an Italian designer who thought himself equal parts artist and carmaker.

Ettore Bugatti wanted to create art on wheels and many would agree that he was the first to go from making race cars to defining the luxury automobile. The first Bugattis were race cars, and their racing models won many early prestigious races, including the 1926 French Grand Prix.

The popular Bugatti race cars led the company to produce a car for the public market. Type 55 was the first street-legal Bugatti, modeled after the Type 51 race car. It had an 8-cylinder engine that could pull 130 horsepower. Onlookers of the late 1930s were amazed at its ability to go from 0 to 60 mph (0 to 97 km/h) in 13 seconds and reach speeds of 115 mph (185 km/h).

The original price of the car was $7,500, which would be $141,000 in today's dollars.

Bugatti's original factory was destroyed early in World War II during a bombing campaign.

BUGATTI MASTERS

1939 was the last year the 24 Hours of Le Mans race was held before the end of World War II. A French driver in a Bugatti Type 57 won the race.

That driver was Jean-Pierre Wimille. During the war, he and two other popular drivers joined the French Resistance. Wimille was the only one to survive.

Major Pre-WW II European Grand Prix wins for Bugatti automobiles:

Year	Country	Event	Driver	Car
1926	France	French Grand Prix	Jules Goux	Type 39 A
1926	Italy	Italian Grand Prix	Louis Charavel	Type 39 A
1926	Spain	Spanish Grand Prix	Bartolomeo Costantini	Type 39 A
1927	Italy	Italian Grand Prix	Tazio Nuvolari	Type 35 C
1928	France	French Grand Prix	William Grover-Williams	Type 35 C
1928	Italy	Italian Grand Prix	Louis Chiron	Type 35 C
1928	Spain	Spanish Grand Prix	Louis Chiron	Type 35 C
1929	France	French Grand Prix	William Grover-Williams	Type 35 B
1929	Germany	German Grand Prix	Louis Chiron	Type 35 B
1929	Spain	Spanish Grand Prix	Louis Chiron	Type 35 B
1929	Monaco	Monaco Grand Prix	William Grover-Williams	Type 35 B
1930	Belgium	Belgian Grand Prix	Louis Chiron	Type 35 C
1930	Czechoslovakia	Czechoslovakian Grand Prix	Heinrich-Joachim von Morgen and Hermann zu Leiningen	Type 35 C
1930	France	French Grand Prix	Philippe Étancelin	Type 35 C
1930	Monaco	Monaco Grand Prix	René Dreyfus	Type 35 C
1931	Belgium	Belgian Grand Prix	William Grover-Williams and Caberto Conelli	Type 35C
1931	Czechoslovakia	Czechoslovakian Grand Prix	Louis Chiron	Type 51
1931	France	French Grand Prix	Louis Chiron and Achille Varzi	Type 51
1931	Monaco	Monaco Grand Prix	Louis Chiron	Type 51
1932	Czechoslovakia	Czechoslovakian Grand Prix	Louis Chiron	Type 51
1933	Czechoslovakia	Czechoslovakian Grand Prix	Louis Chiron	Type 51
1933	Monaco	Monaco Grand Prix	Achille Varzi	Type 51
1934	Belgium	Belgian Grand Prix	René Dreyfus	Type 51
1936	France	French Grand Prix	Jean-Pierre Wimille and Raymond Sommer	Type 57 G

Talbot Lago

Talbot Lago started as a French company founded by Alexandre Darracq in 1896. His name fell off of the cars about eight years after he sold the business in 1912. The group that bought the company also bought Clément-Talbot Limited, a car manufacturer in London, in 1919. The cars were branded Talbot-Darracq until the next year, when Darracq was dropped. When The Great Depression hit, the company struggled financially, and was sold to managing

The 1937 Talbot-Lago T150 SS Teardrop Coupe is the classic pre-war model from this carmaker.

director Antonio Lago in 1936. It was Lago, an engineer by training, who developed a high performing 4L engine from the standard six-cylinder engine.

From 1935 until the start of World War II, Talbot-Lago made some of the most interesting luxury cars. For this carmaker, the pre-war years, 1935–1940, yielded a total of 13 models across four chassis. By comparison, Rolls-Royce had three models during this period, not counting government vehicles.

The most luxurious of the Talbot-Lago cars of this period was the now classic T150 "Teardrop," one of which (a 1937 CSS coupe) sold at a Sotheby's auction in Italy for more than $4.4 million in 2017.

During this pre-war period, it was pretty obvious that the way to get into the luxury car making market was to first make a car that was successful on the race track. The path still holds true today, though to a far lesser degree, as many carmakers now aim first and foremost at the luxury market, bypassing the race car part of the process.

By the early 1940s countries in North America, Asia, Europe, and Africa were involved directly in World War II, and most governments instructed companies to cease all or most luxury goods manufacturing. Materials like leather, silk, rubber, and steel were used for the production of weapons, clothing, medicines, and other military needs.

As Britain moved into war mode, Rolls-Royce and several other motor companies began or expanded airplane engine divisions. This put the brakes on numerous race car projects. Also, during this period most races like the 24 Hours of Le Mans were canceled.

The shift in focus from car engines to airplane engines put a strain on makers like Rolls-Royce after the war. As Europe and America tried to return to a more normal mode of life, companies anchored in the war industry had a harder time than emerging competitors.

The nimbler car companies that cropped up after World War II were the carmakers who changed the sport of racing and the world of automobiles in general. Some companies, like Ferrari, had been brewing before the war. Others, like Aston Martin, came out of opportunities found in newspaper classifieds.

The Rolls-Royce engine of a 1940 Hawker Hurricane IIA fighter plane located at the Brooklands Museum in Weybridge, Surrey, England. The company greatly expanded its airplane engine division during World War II.

1. What was the conflict between old money and new money?

2. Who was the "hyphen" in Rolls-Royce, and why was he important?

3. Why did the production of luxury car cease during World War II?

 RESEARCH PROJECT

Not all luxury car manufacturing ended with the war. World leaders still needed to ride in style. Joseph Stalin, leader of the Soviet Union during World War II, rode around in an armored limousine made from a 1937 Packard. Research what other cars, luxury or otherwise, were driven during the war by the leaders of the United States, United Kingdom, Canada, Australia, Germany, Japan, Spain, and others, and make a chart that list your findings.

design
to prepare the preliminary sketch or the plans for (a work to be executed), especially to plan the form and structure (look and feel) of it

kit car
a car that is delivered to the buyer in parts; the buyer puts the car together

post-war era
the period between the end of World War II and the dissolution of the Soviet Union in 1991

sports car
a small, high-powered automobile with long, low lines, usually seating two persons

CHAPTER 3

Post-World War II: The Romance of the Sports Car

In the years after The Great Depression and World War II, an entire generation of Americans and Europeans were experiencing good times for the first time in their adult lives. As cities were rebuilt in Europe and people in North America came home and returned to school or work, people sought new and exciting ways to have fun and express themselves. The **sports car** caught the imagination of a **post-war era** world as an expression of the success that seemed like a universal possibility.

White MGA (Morris Garages) 1950's Roaster classic sports car with wire wheels, head and fog lights, soft top and luggage rack.

Sports cars come in many varieties. Ford Mustangs are considered sports cars. So is the Nissan 370Z. But these cars are in what is called the mid-price range. Everything has an extreme and cars are no different. "Supercar" began as a term applied to extreme and expensive sports cars.

Though the term "sports car" goes back to the 1920s, its use was generally related to racing cars, and not street-legal cars intended for driving on regular roads. No firm definition of the sports car exists, but most definitions have the following consistencies—sports cars are usually aerodynamically shaped (since the 1950s), and have a low center of gravity compared to standard models. Steering and suspension are typically designed for precise control at high speeds.

Sports car racing and ultimately street-legal model development happened differently in North America and Europe. In Canada and the United States, cars developed a distinctly masculine appearance and a testosterone-fueled feel—that "muscle car" look. They featured lots of chrome and large steering wheels.

Watch footage from the 1956 24 Hours of Le Mans race.

South of the border, from 1950 to 1954, Mexico hosted one of the world's most renowned car races, the Carrera Panamericana. This was a south-to-north border race through Mexico on the newly constructed Pan-American Highway. The race lasted five days and is still considered to have been the most dangerous in the world. Twenty-seven people died in the five years of the race. The fatalities included drivers and spectators.

In respect to Europe, where many of the best drivers lived, the 1950 race was considered too far away and too long. It was dominated by American drivers in rugged American cars like Oldsmobiles, Lincolns and Cadillacs. In later years, Europeans driving Ferraris and Mercedes cars had great success. Ultimately, in addition to the danger, the race proved too expensive for the Mexican government. The race was canceled after its fifth year by proclamation of the Mexican president that the goal of publicizing the Pan-American Highway had been accomplished.

In Europe, the design took a more elegant turn in comparison to the brutish American models. Sports cars coming out of Europe had more curves and ornamentation, such as round mirrors.

Lotus

Lotus was a start-up company begun by two English engineers, Colin Chapman and Colin Dare. They got to work in 1952, soon after receiving their engineering degrees from

Clive Chapman, head of Classic Team Lotus, poses with the Lotus 77, a Formula One racing car designed by his father, Lotus founder Colin Chapman, for the 1976 Formula One season.

The 1967 Lotus Elan +2 was the first Lotus vehicle that could be purchased without assembly required.

University College in London. The first company factory was in a barn.

Lotus was the first race car aimed at young drivers looking to build a reputation for little money. The first Lotus cars were **kit cars**. They were delivered as parts. The cars were to be built by the owners. Since most drivers were also mechanics this was a fairly easy task for Lotus' intended audience. As a plus, buying a car in parts avoided a lot of taxes in the United Kingdom.

Lotus began making production cars in the early 1970s. The Lotus Elan + Two was the first car not available as a kit car.

Lotus remains one the more affordable supercars, ranging from $70,000 to $100,000. What the buyer gets for his or her money is one of those incredible driving experiences in which the driver feels one with the car at high speeds. Spending several hundred thousand dollars more may purchase a more prestigious car, and experts make good arguments on the value of the ride at higher prices. But even with that being the case, a Lotus is in the same league as the other extreme cars.

Cobra

Cobra is an iconic sports car that is both American and British. In fact, it's hard to say whether it's more American or more British. The first inklings of the stylings of the iconic MG sports cars began when British carmaker AC wanted a new engine for a two-seat roadster called the Ace. They moved from using an older model BMW engine to a Chrysler engine. This got the curiosity of American race car driver and designer Carroll Shelby.

The 427 AC Cobra was the last model of Shelby's bold experiment. The last one was produced in 1967.

Carroll Shelby started building Cobras with the bodies of the AC Ace and Ford V8 engines in 1962. Later models like this one could go 0 to 60 mph in 4 seconds, blazing fast at that time.

Both the BMW's and the Chrysler's engines were 6-cylinder models. Shelby wanted a version of the AC Ace which would have an 8-cylinder engine. AC was willing to make the car, however, no V8 engine existed that was small and light enough for the AC frame. That is until Ford wanted to compete with the Chevrolet Corvette and offered Shelby access to their new smaller and lighter weight V8.

The cars were built in both the United States and the United Kingdom. Some models were made in the UK minus the engine, which would be installed at Shelby's shop in Los Angeles.

The last of the Cobra models, the 427 (Mark III), can sell today for as much as $1.5 million. The car was built with a big and powerful 427 cubic inch V8 engine that has 425 horsepower and a top speed of 165 mph (266 km/h).

Temptation and the rising popularity of the Cobra got Shelby in trouble in the early 1990s. *The Los Angeles Times* exposed a scheme where Shelby was claiming to be building new Cobra's using a 1965 chassis, but the chassis were actually copies that had been made in California around 1991 and 1992.

STRETCH LUXURY

The 1932 Bugatti Royale models held the Guinness World Record for the longest production car at 252 inches (6,401 mm) until the 2016 Mercedes Maybach Pullman.

Here are the ten longest production cars ever to come off an assembly line:

Vehicle	Year	Length
1. Mercedes-Maybach Pullman	2016	256 in
2. Bugatti Royale Kellner / Weinberger	1932	252 in
3. Cadillac Fleetwood Seventy-Five	1975	252 in
4. Cadillac V-16	1934	240 in
5. Rolls-Royce Phantom	2009	230 in
6. Pontiac Bonneville	1975	234 in
7. Buick Estate	1977	232 in
8. Chrysler Imperial	1956	230 in
9. Oldsmobile 88	1974	227 in
10. Cadillac Fleetwood	1959	225 in (tie)
10. Buick Electra	1960	225 in (tie)

Ferrari

When Enzo Ferrari formed the Scuderia Ferrari racing team and began making his own cars, he never had a street-legal version in mind. His ambition was to create gentlemen's sports cars for field racing. That basically meant making fast cars for rich people to race on their estates, and there was no worry of having to follow regulations for street-legal cars.

Car lovers, however, had a different idea. With legendary successes at many of Europe's most prestigious races, the public demand led Ferrari's parent company, Fiat, produce street-legal versions of their cars.

Ferrari introduced two versions of the 125 Sport in 1947—a street-legal version and a racing version, like this one that won six Grand Prix races.

On March 12, 1947, Enzo Ferrari took the first street-legal Ferrari for a drive on Italian public roads. Around two months later, two racing versions of this car began on the European race circuit. This car was the iconic 125 Sport (shortly replaced by the 159 Sport), with only a suggestion of a windshield. Both the 125 and 159 have basically the same distinct wide cone shape.

The 125 won six of fourteen races that year including the Grand Prix of Rome. The 159 won the 1947 Turin Grand Prix.

By the 1960s, a new type of consumer arrived: young people. For the first time in the Western world, young people had more money than their counterparts in previous generations. Never before had companies actively marketed their products to teenagers or people in their early twenties.

Prior to the generation born after World War II (the Baby Boom generation), young adults were considered mostly a nuisance. They had no money and were just beginning careers. There was little reason to try to sell them anything. That changed after World War II. By the 1960s, most people graduated high school and the barriers to getting into college had never been lower; the earning potential for this age group had never been higher.

Many places where those under eighteen years of age could find part-time work began popping up. For the first time this group of people, or demographic, was able to buy things, or influence people to buy things for them. Companies realized their new buying power and began marketing many different products to them. One of the products that greatly appealed to the men in this age group was the sports car, and carmakers and their advertisers knew it.

Sports cars have made their way into our imaginations. They make appearances in our dreams and our fantasies. They are the cars the heroes and villains drive in television shows and movies—although the bad guy always seems to have the more expensive car. This highly romanticized notion of the sports car is especially strong with young people. Movies and popular culture have often had this kind of influence on tastes and trends. In the 1960s, this was demonstrated by a man named Bond–James Bond.

Over the decades, sports cars have captured the imagination of drivers everywhere.

TEXT-DEPENDENT QUESTIONS

1. What did the term "sports car" refer to in the 1920s?

2. Which American race car driver asked for an 8-cylinder version of the AC Ace?

3. How many races did the Ferrari 125 Sport win in 1947?

RESEARCH PROJECT

Imagine receiving the parts in the mail and putting together an entire automobile. In the early 1960s that was the only way to get a Lotus. Toy model kits used to be extremely popular with kids many decades ago. Hobby stores still carry them today. Discover a little about the work that went into a kit car by finding and putting together a toy model kit.

exploits
striking or notable deeds, feats, or acts

prestige
reputation or influence arising from success, achievement, rank, or other favorable attributes

rationing
a fixed allowance of provisions or food, especially for the military or for civilians during a shortage

spy novel
a fictional form popular from the 1950s to today where the intrigue-heavy plot centers around an undercover government agent, usually male, who acts to protect his country or another person or territory from imminent harm

CHAPTER 4

David Brown: The Man Who Made James Bond's Car

By the 1960s the rumored **exploits** of spies fighting the Cold War gave birth to the **spy novel**. James Bond was the best-known fictional spy, and during the 1960s, the character began appearing in movies. Being in the movies requires glamour, so one of the things James Bond needed was a really knockout car. Of course, since James Bond was a British spy the car needed to be British.

For the films featuring author Ian Fleming's British spy James Bond, the producers wanted a cool car, and Aston Martin was the clear choice.

Aston Martins appear in a total of thirteen James Bond films. He is most often shown driving a DB5.

Film	Year	AM Model	Model Year
Goldfinger	1964	DB5	1963
Thunderball	1965	DB5	1963
On Her Majesty's Secret Service	1969	DB5	1963
Diamonds Are Forever	1971	DBS	1967
The Living Daylights	1987	V8 Vantage Volante	1986
Goldeneye	1995	DB5	1965
Tomorrow Never Dies	1997	DB5	1963
The World is Not Enough	1999	DB5	1963
Die Another Day	2002	V12 Vanquish	2001
Casino Royale	2006	DB5, DBS V12	1963, 2007
Quantum Of Solace	2008	DBS V12	2007
Skyfall	2012	DB5	1963
Spectre	2015	DB10 & DB5	2014 & 1963

Rolls-Royce would have been the obvious choice, but the world was changing in the 1960s, and James Bond needed a fast car with sleek style. Rolls are elegant. They also look out of place chasing evil henchmen down a ski slope. Working in the racing world while overseeing development of the

DB series of car, entrepreneur and designer David Brown gave the Aston Martin a style to match the spy world of the 1960s. Or, at least it was the right car to match the public's imagination of what the spy world was like.

While the Aston Martin brand is associated with power and **prestige**, David Brown was born to a middle-class family near Yorkshire in the United Kingdom. The family owned a gearbox factory founded by David Brown's grandfather, also named David Brown. The company was called David Brown & Sons, and upon the death of the founding David Brown, his sons Percy and Frank took it over. Frank Brown was David's father and he had little interest in cars. His mother, however, was an avid driver and, as a child, rode as a passenger in various test runs of David Brown & Sons' vehicles.

David Brown started working at the family business as just another apprentice. He soon acquired a motorcycle, which eventually led him into racing. His parents, however, were cautious. They would not let him participate as an alternate for a team in a run of the Isle of Man Tourist Trophy race.

David Brown bought Aston Motors for about $55,000 in 1947, and proceeded to make the brand relevant.

He started designing and building his own race cars, one of which reached a speed of 140 mph on a sandy raceway, a unique achievement for a car in the early twentieth century.

After these early exploits on the raceway, David Brown studied business methods and manufacturing techniques around the world. These experiences led him to bring new steel production methods to the UK that created stronger castings for aircraft and heavy equipment. He also founded a tractor company. So far, this is not exactly the stuff of swank and prestige. So, when he saw a classified advertisement in *The London Times* in 1947 offering a "High-Class Motor Business" for sale, few would have guessed he would create one the world's most expensive and elegant car brands.

After World War II, Great Britain was a landscape of bombed-out buildings. What factories were left were geared for war production. Food **rationing** was still going on even though the war had been over for two years.

David Brown bought Aston Motors for around $55,000. They had been a minor race car maker before World War II and the company was pretty much in financial ruin. Within a few years, he was able to add an engine maker (Lagonda) and a carriage maker. With these assets, he built the first DB series of cars, both for the race track and the roadway.

Most of the model names since the David Brown era have had the designation "DB" with an incremental number next to it, i.e. DB1, DB2, DB3, etc. 2016 saw the release of the DB11.

The first car debuted in 1947. The 2-litre Sports DB1 was a two-seater sports car with a relatively small 2L 4-cylinder engine. Even with that small engine, a prototype version won the 24 Hours of Spa race in Belgium in 1948. The road version had a top speed of 90 mph (145 km/h). Only 15 were made.

Aston Martin released the DB11 in 2016.

The DB2 was the breakthrough model for Aston Martin. It debuted at the 1950 New York Auto Show. The car was popular enough to spawn several versions, including a drophead coupe. This model had a V6 Lagonda engine and could reach a top speed of 116 mph (187 km/h).

Introduced in 1951, the DB Mark III (DB3) was essentially a variant of the DB2, one that was available as a hatchback, a somewhat revolutionary design for the time that became common decades later. Other upgrades included the modernization of the instrument panel, brakes, and clutch.

The DB4 debuted in 1958. This version upgraded the engine and offered a GT option with special valves that produced more power, up to about 250 horsepower. This Aston Martin broke the 10-second barrier in the 0 to 60 mph (0 to 92 km/h) category.

The next Aston Martin became the most recognizable. The DB5, released in 1963, was the car made famous by the James Bond films. This was the first Aston Martin to come standard with a 4L engine and a five-speed transmission. The special Vantage engine upgrade could produce more than 300 horsepower.

Brown had a special version of the DB5 made for himself. While controversial today and illegal in most of the United Kingdom, fox hunting was once a popular and legal pastime

The classic DB2 Debuted at the 1950 New York Auto Show.

The DB5, the James Bond Aston Martin, is the brand's most recognizable model.

and David Brown's favorite sport. Called a "shooting brake," his version of the DB5 had an extended cab for carrying guns and dogs on a hunt.

The DB6 was one of the last cars overseen by David Brown. Production lasted longer than any previous model, from 1965 to 1971. When the car premiered at the London Motor Show, most reviews commented on its dated style, which looked very much like the DB5. The major cosmetic differences were in the length of the car and the styling of the wheels and bumpers. Under the hood, the car had pretty much the same specs as the DB5, though the DB6 did come available in a 3-speed automatic transmission.

See the actual Aston Martin used in Goldfinger, complete with props.

The last car overseen by David Brown was the DBS, a V8 Aston Martin produced from 1967 to 1972. The car was featured in the James Bond movie *On Her Majesty's Secret Service*.

By 1972, Aston Martin was caught in a European recession and looked like it might not survive financially. David Brown managed to pay off the company's debts and sold Aston Martin in 1972 for £101, or about $280. The company floated between different owners for about a decade before being taken over by Ford Motor Company in 1991. Today, several larger companies own Aston Martin with Ford still owning a substantial stake in the company. Daimler AG also owns a stake in Aston Martin.

Aston Martsin has been one of the most influential car brands if not one of the most widely known. Anyone who ever owned a Ford Taurus can thank Aston Martin for the car's curved look, something that turned heads back in the early 1990s.

The DBS is the last model personally overseen by David Brown.

TEXT-DEPENDENT QUESTIONS

1. Where was David Brown born?

2. Where did David Brown find out the Aston Martin company was for sale?

3. Which company took control of Aston Martin in 1991?

 # RESEARCH PROJET

James Bond drove other cars too. In fact, carmakers have gone to great lengths to get their cars in the films. Do some research and make a chart listing all the other cars that have appeared in James Bond films; see if you can find the answer to why there were AMC cars in Bond films.

drag racing
a first-across-the-finish-line race, usually between two cars, from a standing start over a measured distance down a straight pathway

hybrid
a car or other vehicle that combines an internal-combustion engine with one or more electric motors powered by a battery

supercar
an exotic car with both high-end luxury and performance

CHAPTER 5

Michelle Christensen: Exotic Car Designer of the Future

Beginning in the 1950s, California was booming, and it attracted people from all walks of life who came west to chase their dreams. Those who aspired to be in films came to Hollywood. Those who wanted to build rockets went to work at Jet Propulsion Laboratory in Pasadena. If someone wanted to race cars they came to California for its racing circuit.

Before the endless housing developments and shopping centers spread across southern California, racetracks dotted the landscape. From Eureka to San Diego, racetracks and drag strips were about as common as movie theaters—every

In the 1950s and '60s, racetracks dotted the landscape in Southern California.

city had at least one. While many of these tracks have closed over the years, some remain in operation today. California still has a thriving racing culture.

Out of this community came one of the auto industry's top designers, and her recent work has helped bring the latest **hybrid** power technology to the **supercar** world.

SOCAL SPEED

More auto races have been held in Southern California than in any other location in the world. The region has been home to 174 racetracks, the first of which opened in 1903.

Cliff Durant, a famous race car driver of the early twentieth century, built what was the fastest race track in the world in Beverly Hills, CA. The track opened in 1920, and though successful, closed in 1924, as the Beverly Hills land was more profitable as space for movie stars' homes.

Michelle Christensen grew up going to car shows and drag racing tracks with her father.

Watch an interview with Michelle Christensen via Motorweek.

Michelle Christensen had a really cool upbringing and it is not surprising that she became professionally interested in creating supercars. Her dad was one of the best car designers ever. He was a race car maker and driver, and he included his daughter in his interest in cars and **drag racing**. From a young age, Christensen began helping her father in his shop.

Her childhood, as she put it to *Design Boom*, "was a blur of car shows, drag races, and loud engine noises, early on Saturday mornings." Christensen remembers sitting on a crate in the hollowed out interior of a car as her father rebuilt it. As she got older she got more hands-on, helping him fix cars.

Before Christensen knew that car design was a possible career path, she was creating and designing things, including a prom dress for a friend. The feeling of creating something with an emotional attachment led her into the field of design. At a car show with her father, she learned that there was such a job as a car designer. It was then and there that Christensen knew her future direction.

She attended and graduated from the Art Center College of Design in Pasadena, CA. There her outstanding drawings got the attention of Honda where she went to work for their Acura brand as a designer.

The first generation Honda NSX was produced from 1990 to 2005. In 2011 the company announced plans to build a successor.

CRUISER CONTROL

The Art Center College of Design in Pasadena, CA, had another famous car designer graduate besides Michelle Christensen. Bryan Nesbitt is best known as the designer of the Chrysler PT Cruiser. Popular in the early 2000s, the PT Cruiser was a family car with a twist. The exterior design gave the car both a futuristic and a classic 1950s station wagon look, like what someone might drive to go surfing on Mars. Over 1.3 million PT Cruisers were made between 2001 and 2010.

When Honda's American division confirmed in December 2007 that a new ten-valve supercar would be produced, Christensen was already working at Honda. In fact, her drawing won the company's exterior design competition. That particular car was in production by 2010, but

Unlike the first generation NSX which was manufactured in Japan, the new NSX was designed and engineered in Marysville, OH, at Honda's plant, by designer Michelle Christensen and chief engineer Ted Klaus.

development never got beyond prototypes made in 2008. Instead, Honda scrapped the project, with the company CEO stating that "due to poor economic conditions, . . . all plans for a next-generation NSX had been canceled."

Then in 2011, Honda announced new plans to build a successor to the NSX. In a story by *Automobile*, Honda's CEO stated the car would be exhilarating to drive, but also environmentally friendly. That drawing from several years before, which won Christensen Honda's in-house competition, remained the exterior design model for the new NSX, and she was made lead designer on the project.

Christensen approached designing the NSX from the point of view of the driver. Creating the look and feel of the car then became a job of making sure all instrumentation and controls were placed so the driver could intuitively find them.

The NSX Christensen designed was the second generation NSX. The first NSX was sold from 1990 to 2005. She calls her design a new esthetic to reflect a new era. Though in contrast, some features, like wide rear taillights, are a nod to the original NSX.

Her goal is to make driving and operating a car a seamless experience. Christensen said in an interview to *Gear Patrol*, "good design is something that envelops you, to the point that you don't even really know it's there." She went on to describe how many times the end user of a product is not aware of the design that went into it. Christensen said, "That's why we enjoy certain experiences so much more, regardless of whether they're houses, cars, or other products."

The Acura NSX has a unique hybrid system of gas and electric motors. Car and Driver magazine called the NSX, "a rolling test bed for the future of performance technology." The Acura uses an electric motor for the car's drivetrain.

The top speed of the NSX is 191 mph and the car can go from 0 to 60 mph (km) in 3.0 seconds.

The taillights of the second generation NSX are a nod to the original.

TEXT-DEPENDENT QUESTIONS

1. When did Michelle Christensen decide she wanted to design cars?

2. What model did Christensen design for Honda's Acura brand?

3. How does Christensen describe "good design"?

 # RESEARCH PROJECT

Try out what it's like to design something. Use perhaps an appliance in your home, or the family car, for example. Draw a diagram with an accompanying report on how the product could be made better. Things to pay attention to would be ease of use, safety, and overall function of the product.

body
the section of a vehicle, usually in the shape of a box, cylindrical container, or platform, in or on which passengers or the load is carried

metal foam
solid aluminum with gas-filled pores that enables increased energy absorption during collisions

prototype
a car created to serve as a demonstration of design ideas, but which does not yet have certain essential features like an engine

CHAPTER 6

Today's Superstar Exotic Cars

Today the automotive industry is changing the most since the end of World War II. Electric and other alternatives power sources are making their way into the marketplace and even Mercedes plans an electric supercar to be widely available around 2020.

Materials like stretchable metals are planned to be in use by 2018, making one potential supercar virtually indestructible. Numerous newcomers from Poland and Mexico will try to bring their cars to the market and racing circuits.

Here are a number of the cars, some of which definitely will, and others of which might or might not, make an impact among exotic car owners and enthusiasts.

Bugatti Veyron luxury sport car on display in New York.

The Bugatti Chiron boasts an 8.0L W16 quad-turbocharged engine that goes 0 to 60 mph in 2.4 seconds.

Bugatti Chiron

Bugatti very well may become the company that directs the future of exotic car design. They will be premiering the new Chiron next year, and it is an amazing car. Bugatti will replace its current flagship model, the Veyron, with the Chiron.

The Chiron will continue the Bugatti tradition of sporting an 8L W16 quad-turbocharged engine, although the new version has been tweaked for more power. The Chiron's engine will have roughly twenty percent more power than the Veyron. It will be able to go from 0 to 60 mph (0 to 97 km) in 2.4 seconds. Even at a base price of $2.5 million, the first 200 cars sold before the first one was completed.

The Koenigsegg CCRX Trevita is the most expensive street-legal production car in the world at $4.8 million. The car is literally covered in diamonds, and not for show. A diamond dust resin is used to coat the car to make the body resist scratches. At that price, no one wants to get dinged in a parking lot.

Koenigsegg produced only two Trevitas. The car pulls about 1.5Gs (1½ times Earth gravity) as it goes from 0 to 60 mph (0 to 97 km) in 2.9 seconds. At a top speed of 410 mph, the Trevita might not be street-legal in the United States. While American boxing champion Floyd Mayweather Jr. purchased one of these two treasured cars, it is unknown whether he ever got a license plate for it. Often owners of supercars only drive them on private roads and race tracks. As of July 2017, Floyd Mayweather's Trevita was up for sale.

The Arrinera Hussarya is the first modern Polish supercar.

Arinera Hussarya

Arinera Hussarya is an intriguing new brand that may make supercar status. Arinera is the first car manufacturer out of Poland to produce racing **prototypes**. These were introduced in 2011, and the company expects to announce a 2018 production schedule for a street-legal version.

However, controversy has surrounded the carmaker as they have moved up their production schedule numerous times since 2011. Some have challenged the company's claim that their automobile is truly original and not a reworked kit car.

Ferrari LaFerrari

This will be one of the first hybrids available from Ferrari, with more power than any other Ferrari while reducing fuel consumption by 40 percent.

The car has a 6.3L V12 engine, electric motor, and a KERS unit pulsing short bursts of extra power. With a top speed of 217 mph (349 km/h), Ferrari announced the LaFerrari holds the internal lap record over any previous Ferrari automobile.

FERRARI THE BEAUTIFUL

In 2014, Ferrari celebrated sixty years in North America by creating a special model, the Ferrari F60 America. Production of the car was a secret as they built just ten of these star-and-stripes-themed car, which of course, was a convertible. All ten were offered exclusively to Ferrari's top customers. Every one of them was sold before the cars were made or even announced.

Chevrolet Corvette Z06 2018

Chevrolet has made some very cool changes in the new Corvette. Panels made from a carbon nanocomposite make up part of the underbody. These panels help with the dynamic balance of the car. Dynamic balance has to do with how the car keeps its center of gravity while moving. A better dynamic balance means a more comfortable ride when driving into turns at high speeds.

One design change in the Corvette Z06 has caused some controversy. Car lovers usually adore the trademark aspects of a particular brand or model. The Cobra has its roll bar. Rolls-Royce has its grill. And Corvette has its taillights. In the new Z06, the taillights have gone from the trademark round shape to a more angular, square-like shape.

Although it is a hybrid, Ferrari boasts that its LaFerrari is the most powerful car it has ever produced.

Watch the latest teaser for the Inferno Exotic Car.

Chevrolet will also be reviving the Stingray name, last used in 1976. So the Corvette Z06 will also be known as a Corvette Stingray. Chevrolet announced the C7 Z06 at the 2014 Detroit Auto Show.

Inferno

Mexico has been developing a supercar industry that has been building for about decade. Soon, a game-changing car out of Mexico may someday influence how all cars are made. Currently, Mexican companies are making supercars like the Mastretta MXT and the Vuhl 05. These cars are currently in production and getting generally positive feedback from reviewers.

Now comes a new supercar out of Mexico constructed with a revolutionary material. The Inferno is an exotic car like no other. What covers the Inferno is what's so special and futuristic about it. The car utilizes what is being called **metal foam**. It's a combination of zinc, aluminum, and silver that stretches upon impact. The car's skin can withstand an impact similar to that of an armored vehicle.

If true to its maker's claim, the Inferno will be a game-changing car. The Inferno model name is simply "Exotic Car." That's right, its name is the Inferno Exotic Car. It is expected to have 1,400 horsepower that will take the car from 0 to 60 mph in less than 2.7 seconds. That will be amazing and far outstrip other street-legal cars in terms of how many horses are under the hood.

The car is expected to be available in 2018 and has been

shown in various concept stages at car shows since 2015. However, even great ideas and proven research do not guarantee a company will be successful. Prototype vehicles like the Inferno often never got off the ground. Such is the fate of many start-ups. They can get a great idea from the drawing board to the lab, but no further. But if the Inferno does happen and the car's physical capabilities meet the hype, the Inferno should change how every car is made.

Vuhl

The VUHL 05 is Mexico's latest sports car in full production. The car was introduced in London in 2013 and after several years of testing production started in Mexico in 2015.

The car can go from 0 to 60 mph (0 to 97 km) in 2.6 seconds and reach a top speed of 160 mph (257 km). Like with the Inferno, the VUHL has an exterior made from unique materials. The **body** is constructed with plastic and carbon fibers.

Race of Champions selected Mexico's VUHL 05 as the partner for its world's best driver event in Miami.

Mercedes "Project One"

In late 2017, Mercedes announced plans for a hybrid supercar for 2019 that will cost $2.7 million. "Project One" is the working name of the car, though the final model name will surely be something flashier. It will have a relatively small turbocharged V6 engine, but that engine will be supplemented with a 161 horsepower electric motor. The configuration of the car and the engineering of the motors have been developed from years of racing research. As of late 2017, Mercedes says that all of the 275 incomplete "Project One" cars that they plan on making already have been sold.

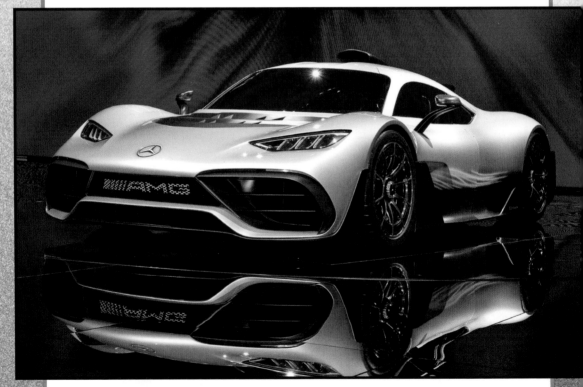

The Mercedes "Project One" concept car gleams at its world premiere at the Frankfurt International Motor Show in September 2017.

TEXT-DEPENDENT QUESTIONS

1. How did Ferrari celebrate their 60th anniversary of selling cars in North America?

2. What is special about the body material of the Inferno Exotic Car?

3. Which supercar will be a hybrid (using electric and gas motors)?

RESEARCH PROJET

Many exciting supercars are on the drawing board right now. These cars will use various hybrid or purely electric motors to power the vehicle. Go to the websites of the carmakers in this book and look for a section called "Press Room" or something similar. This will be where announcements are kept. Make a list of alternative power concept cars that are currently in development.

Series Glossary of Terms

Aerodynamic Drag
Drag produced by a moving object as it displaces the air in its path. Aerodynamic drag is a force usually measured in pounds; it increases in proportion to the object's frontal area, its drag coefficient, and the square of its speed.

Ball Joint
A flexible joint consisting of a ball in a socket, used primarily in front suspensions because it can accommodate a wide range of angular motion.

Camshaft
A shaft fitted with several cams, whose lobes push on valve lifters to convert rotary motion into linear motion. One or more camshafts regulate the opening and closing of the valves in all piston engines.

Carbon Fiber
Threadlike strands of pure carbon that are extremely strong in tension (that is, when pulled) and are reasonably flexible. Carbon fiber can be bound in a matrix of plastic resin by heat, vacuum, or pressure to form a composite that is strong and light—and very expensive.

Chassis
A general term that refers to all of the mechanical parts of a car attached to a structural frame. In cars with unitized construction, the chassis comprises everything but the body of the car.

Cylinder
The round, straight-sided cavity in which the pistons move up and down. Typically made of cast iron and formed as a part of the block.

Differential
A special gearbox designed so that the torque fed into it is split and delivered to two outputs that can turn at different speeds. Differentials within axles are designed to split torque evenly; however, when used between the front and rear axles in four-wheel-drive systems (a center differential), they can be designed to apportion torque unevenly.

Drivetrain
All of a car's components that create power and transmit it to the wheels; i.e. the engine, the transmission, the differential(s), the hubs, and any interconnecting shafts.

Fuel Injection
Any system that meters fuel to an engine by measuring its needs and then regulating the fuel flow, by electronic or mechanical means, through a pump and injectors. Throttle-body injection locates the injector(s) centrally in the throttle-body housing, while port injection allocates at least one injector for each cylinder near its intake port.

Horsepower
The common unit of measurement of an engine's power. One horsepower equals 550 foot-pounds per second, the power needed to lift 550 pounds one foot off the ground in one second: or one pound 550 feet up in the same time.

Intake Manifold
The network of passages that direct air or air-fuel mixture from the throttle body to the intake ports in the cylinder head. The flow typically proceeds from the throttle body into a chamber called the plenum, which in turn feeds individual tubes, called runners, leading to each intake port. Engine breathing is enhanced if the intake manifold is configured to optimize the pressure pulses in the intake system.

Overdrive

Any gearset in which the output shaft turns faster than the input shaft. Overdrive gears are used in most modern transmissions because they reduce engine rpm and improve fuel economy.

Overhead Cam

The type of valvetrain arrangement in which the engine's camshaft(s) is in its cylinder head(s). When the camshaft(s) is placed close to the valves, the valvetrain components can be stiffer and lighter, allowing the valves to open and close more rapidly and the engine to run at higher rpm. In a single-overhead-cam (SOHC) layout, one camshaft actuates all of the valves in a cylinder head. In a double-overhead-camshaft (DOHC) layout, one camshaft actuates the intake valves, and one camshaft operates the exhaust valves.

Powertrain

An engine and transmission combination.

Rack-and-Pinion

A steering mechanism that consists of a gear in mesh with a toothed bar, called a ""rack."" The ends of the rack are linked to the steered wheels with tie rods. When the steering shaft rotates the gear, it moves the rack from side to side: turning the wheels.

Sedan

As used by *Car and Driver*, the term "sedan" refers to a fixed-roof car with at least four doors or any fixed-roof two-door car with at least 33 cubic feet of rear interior volume, according to measurements based on SAE standard J1100.

Shock Absorber

A device that converts motion into heat, usually by forcing oil through small internal passages in a tubular housing. Used primarily to dampen suspension oscillations, shock absorbers respond to motion.

Spoiler

An aerodynamic device that changes the direction of airflow in order to reduce lift or aerodynamic drag and/or improve engine cooling.

Supercharger

An air compressor used to force more air into an engine than it can inhale on its own. The term is frequently applied only to mechanically driven compressors, but it actually encompasses all varieties of compressors.

Turbocharger

A supercharger powered by an exhaust-driven turbine. Turbochargers always use centrifugal-flow compressors, which operate efficiently at the high rotational speeds produced by the exhaust turbine.

Source: caranddriver.com

FURTHER READING

Brun, Frederic. *James Bond Cars*. London: Aurum, 2015.

Cockerham, Paul W. *Rolls-Royce and Bentley: Classic Elegance.* New York: New Line Books, 2005.

Laban, Brian. *Le Mans - 24 Hours: The Complete Story of the World's Most Famous Motor Race.* London: Virgin Books, 2001.

Master, Matt. *Top Gear: The Cool 500: The Coolest Cars Ever Made.* London: BBC Books, 2013.

Stevenson, Heon. *British Car Advertising of the 1960s.* Jefferson: McFarland, 2016.

INTERNET RESOURCES

http://www.motorweek.org/

The website for television's longest running automotive series. It features videos of test drives and comparison tests of many exotic cars.

http://dragstriplist.com/

An encyclopedia of United States drag strip history.

http://www.designboom.com/

A website for information and resources on the profession of design.

http://www.motorsportmagazine.com/

A website for Motor Sport Magazine, one of racing's most respected publications. Their website contains an archive of nearly a century of their publishing history.

http://www.celebritycarblog.com

A long-running and popular blog about celebrities and their automobiles.

EDUCATIONAL VIDEO CREDITS:

Chapter 1: http://x-qr.net/1D1G

Chapter 2: http://x-qr.net/1FbZ

Chapter 3: http://x-qr.net/1D5A

Chapter 4: http://x-qr.net/1FeF

Chapter 5: http://x-qr.net/1Do2

Chapter 6: http://x-qr.net/1D3P

PHOTO CREDITS:

INDEX

INDEX

INDEX

AUTHOR'S BIOGRAPHY

Norm Geddis lives in Southern California where he works as a writer, video editor, and collectibles expert. He once spent two years cataloging and appraising over one million old movie props. He is currently restoring film and video content from the 1950's DuMont Television Network for the Days of DuMont channel on Roku.